The Global Chameleon

How to excel in international sales

BY

VINCENT S. DANIELS, © 2004

Acknowledgements

This book is dedicated to my wife Marianne, who supported me in my desire to be a successful international businessman, in spite of the time spent away traveling the world. I also dedicate this book to my sons Jonathan and Sebastian for growing up with a part-time father.

I would also like to acknowledge several people without whom this book would have withered in the brain and never been put into print: Kathryn Morris for editing the manuscript; Bill Voris and Roy Herberger, Presidents of Thunderbird, the Garvin School of International Management; professors and friends at Thunderbird, especially Paul Johnson; my colleague Grisell Sotolongo; Ken Roberts, editor at WorldCity Business for his encouragement, suggestions and deadlines; and finally to Sister Mary Scholastica and Sister Mary Michael of Saint Frances de Chantal school in the Bronx for teaching me to write in the first place.

Table Of Contents

Preface

Some years ago I began writing a series of articles for a Miami international trade publication, WorldCity Business. The editor, Ken Roberts was kind enough to give me the moniker "The Global Salesman". This year I decided to edit and compile these articles into the book that you are currently reading.

Several of the chapters refer to Miami and Florida as part of the story line. Although Miami is mentioned in these chapters, they are applicable to any major city. In fact the first chapter, "The Export Market" was initially written about the New York export market. For WorldCity I modified it to reflect the Miami marketplace. I use the feminine and masculine pronouns interchangeably in these articles.

Since leaving the business world in 1999 I have taught many classes in marketing and sales. I was very surprised that there were virtually no books devoted to the subject of international sales or international selling. I hope that this book, "The Global Chameleon" will fill that void and help many business people learn to excel in international sales.

The Export Market

Toward the end of last year I received a "Special Issue" of Miami Business magazine. This issue was named "The Power Issue" and it highlighted the 100 most powerful people in Miami. As I perused it, my thought was, "all the usual suspects". It listed realtors, lawyers, politicians, heads of NGOs, and a few bankers—virtually all service industry luminaries!

I was puzzled. Where were the exporters, heads of Latin American sales offices, freight forwarders and customs house brokers, leaders of major regional offices with warehousing and purchasing in Miami? The real "powerful" people in Miami were hardly even mentioned. However, after 24 years as a part of the Miami business community, I realize that this is not a new phenomenon. The real international business community in Miami is very often ignored by the media and, often, by the rest of Miami. They are stealth players, rarely taking part in the local power game, concentrating instead on developing business, hiring people and generating income for themselves and their companies. In other words, being the true power generators of the Miami area.

These companies also serve as a strong market for the local providers of goods and services. They are a market that most manufacturers, distributors and agents, should be paying attention to. As an example, I owned a heavy equipment distribution company from 1980 to 1995 with a facility west of the Miami International Airport, where many of these companies tend to settle. In 15 years, I never had one lawyer or accountant come calling on me for business. A lone banker was smart enough to hand-deliver a letter of credit. A couple of years later, because of that small attention paid to service, I obtained a mortgage for my building from him. These 'forgotten' companies are large users of local services and products, and an under tapped local market.

These companies can also serve as an important funnel for global sales, serving as a gateway into new markets.

They fall into three categories of export companies:

- The U. S. purchasing office of a domestic company with overseas operations
- The U. S. purchasing office of a foreign company
- An Exporter

The Overseas Purchasing Office of a U.S. Company

Perhaps you are already selling to the first category: U.S. companies with foreign operations or sales. Many major and minor corporations have overseas operations, and do their purchasing through a Miami office. If so, you have the opportunity to learn, and to expand your export sales. Visit with the people responsible for the export purchasing. Become familiar with the terminology. Visit the library and research the destination market. If you are already serving a foreign market through U.S. companies, you may have a built in introduction to other firms in the same country. Once you have built a relationship with the company, you may want to pay a courtesy visit to your customer's overseas operation, and perhaps gain an introduction to other potential customers.

You may be dealing with American nationals as purchasing agents in these companies. Chances are they will not speak the language of the client country. Most of these professional purchasing agents are college graduates who have little technical knowledge of all the products they buy. Take some time to educate these purchasing agents about the technical aspects of your product and you will have made a friend and, more importantly, a bonafide step toward a valued business relationship.

What these purchasing agents do know are sources, perhaps competitors, and other purchasing agents. Ask for referrals! And while you are giving them product knowledge, ask questions about shipping, marketing, problems, pleasures, customs and anything else to do with exporting.

One advantage of dealing with this kind of company is familiarity. They are listed in trade directories. Dun and Bradstreet knows them. Information regarding reputation and creditworthiness is easily available. This may not be true of companies in the other two categories of export companies.

The U.S. Purchasing Office of a Foreign Company

Large foreign companies often rely heavily on products from the United States and other major manufacturing countries. These products may be high-tech products, heavy equipment, medical products, raw materials or disposable diapers. The product mix is limited only by the gap between what we produce and what their home country does not.

If the company produces an exportable commodity, these foreign purchasing offices may be co-located with a U.S. sales office, which may also be located in Miami, Texas, California or the New York area. Again, get to the library and do your research! Also, refer to trade associations and journals. You will find lists of natural resource companies, breweries, farms, factories and all manner of prospective clients for your business/product.

In these, you will find a greater mix of nationals from the client country. They will most likely be very familiar with English and American business customs. You will still find the American purchasing agent, but there is a better chance that he speaks the language, or has visited the company's home country. The higher-level managers will very often be nationals of the home country. Here is your opportunity to leverage your knowledge of foreign languages and customs or become motivated to do so.

You will undoubtedly have the opportunity to meet with, and perhaps have lunch with, the foreign managers. Do not be afraid to ask questions about his home country and company. He will probably be pleased that you are interested. But, do your homework first! Get back to the library! Learn about his country before you ask questions. Study the map of the country, and be familiar with the main cities and industrial centers. Try to learn some of the history. Then you will be prepared to ask intelligent questions, and you will gain his respect. Even more importantly, you will have expanded your horizons. It is amazing how one good order can increase one's interest in geography and history!

The Exporter

These are the "five percenters" that the U. S. manufacturers love to hate because they steal sales from overseas distributors, and generally mess up the distribution network that the manufacturer has worked for years to build. My question to the manufacturers is, if your network is so good, why do the so-called "five percenters" exist?

I'll go a step further and say that this is the international free market working at its best.

The exporter is generally a small company. It may consist of an individual working from his home. After all, the first rule of the exporter is "keep the overhead low". He probably started the company with little or no money. More than likely, he will not last in business more than a few years. The chances are great that he is a native of his customer's country. He probably relies on contacts back home, and may have only one or two clients. The business is risky, so be careful.

But, as with any risky business, there are opportunities. Export orders can often be quite large, and payment terms quite secure. You will not have too much of a chance to learn about exporting from an exporter. He will be paranoid that you will be trying to contact his client directly. And he may be right.

Try to deal with exporters who have been in business for three or more years and who have good references and reasonable financial statements. An exporter who sells two or three million dollars of product a year may only be worth twenty thousand dollars on the books.

The key is determining if he is legitimate and intends to stay in business, and that his clients have good payment records. If you have to bid ten quotes to get one order. If he tries to get you to lower your prices and improve your deliveries, and calls every other day, you may not want to do business with him. And, of course, you want the orders to be large enough to justify the work.

Many exporters have strange financial statements, and, unlike the readers of this article, hate to pay taxes. I once had an exporter ask me for an open account. His financial statements showed a loss for his first year in business, and a negative net worth. When I asked him about this, he lowered his voice and confided that he makes most of his profits in Panama. I declined his request. I later discovered that he had two previous companies; both of them had gone bankrupt. I wonder how wealthy his Panamanian company is, at the expense of his trusting suppliers. The key is to check the exporter out thoroughly. Do not give him an open account unless he is trustworthy and has a good history.

How can you secure payment? This is not as difficult a proposition as you may suspect. Ask for a letter of credit. Quite often, his client is opening a letter of credit, and he can get a back-to-back. An easier method, if you are convinced that he is a reliable exporter, is to take an assignment of his letter of credit. As long as he gets his paperwork right, you will get paid. I will reserve a greater discussion of international financial rules and definitions to a later article. Although it is a simple procedure, the process can be as intricate as a master's chess match.

The Key to Great Global Sales

Time and distance are the most important differences between local and global selling. Years ago, when I started my first company in central New Jersey, most of my clients were local, situated in neighboring Manhattan; these clients were the purchasing officers of major foreign companies, specifically mining companies. Because the purchasing offices were close by, it was easy for me to follow up on a sales call or to drop by again the week after the call with a price quote.

In global sales, though, a salesperson does not have that luxury; he or she has to make the best use of time because the distance is so great. After my first few international sales trips, I realized that I had to change my approach; I had to plan more carefully. I remember an early trip to Bolivia. I called my clients and a host of prospects to advise them of my impending visit and to set up appointments. They were all very positive and, except for a firm appointment with one client, asked me to call as soon as I arrived. I arrived in La Paz on a Sunday and began calling everyone on Monday. They were all busy but "would return my call." I visited my one client and waited for the return calls.

I also waited all day Tuesday and read a great Michener novel to pass the time. On Wednesday, I began to panic and to call the prospects again. Again, they said they would return my calls. And they did. On Thursday! And they all wanted to meet on Friday. That was impossible, although I tried my best. That experience taught me lesson number one in international sales—namely, that time is of a premium. Now, I force the issue with clients as far as I can and set up visits before I leave home.

Because I had the opportunity to visit Bolivia only twice a year, the distance factor made the time factor crucial. Unlike in local sales, I couldn't simply return the next week to continue a sales call. Planning became mandatory in order for me to be able to make the best use of my valuable time and to insure a good outcome from my visits.

Another imperative to insuring a good outcome in global selling is what I call that the "advance agreement." It is a move that tends to separate the 'great' global salespeople from the rest. Most good salespeople try to set an agenda with the client or prospect before or while scheduling the visit. Great salespeople, however, also try to set the outcome of the meeting in advance of the visit. In essence, this means closing the sale before the meeting takes place.

A good advance agreement has several key elements. The amount of detail required for each element depends on the nature of the product or service being sold and the level of trust the salesperson has built with the client.

Suppose you are the good salesperson who wants to be 'great'. There are some steps you can follow secure a good outcome by actively seeking an advance agreement.

1. The first step in securing an advance agreement is to establish the topics to be discussed during the meeting. You may do it verbally or in writing, but with email being so pervasive, writing is the better medium.

2. After setting up the topics, you should describe your role in the meeting. This step can be a simple as stating that you will have questions to ask about the sale—

such as potential problems, budget, and the decision process. It also can be a more complicated formula. Perhaps you will have to have meetings scheduled with managers and users, with financial people, or with others. You will have to ask all of them a set of pertinent questions. Maybe you also will need access to a work site or computer program. You may even have to install something for testing and need prior consent to do so. Whatever your role is going to be in the visit, spell it out.

3. Once you have established your role, you have to identify the role and expectations you have of the client. Certainly, you have to give permission for the client to ask any pertinent questions, but the client's role may go beyond that. It may be that the client has to bring something to the meeting–drawings, statistics, or other data. He or she may have to set up internal meetings or arrange for a company plane to take you to a work site. Whatever roles the client has to play in order to make your sales visit a success, spell those out as well.

4. The next element is to establish a mutual understanding of the next step in the process and agree to move to that next step if certain goals are met during your visit. You are giving the client permission to say "Yes". You also have to give the client permission to say "No" if the goals of the visit are not met or if there is no match between your company's abilities and their needs. There is nothing worse—or more expensive—in global sales than "beating a dead horse". If it makes

no sense to continue the dialogue, the most professional move a salesman can make is to focus on a better prospect. Of course, be sure to get a referral before you move forward.

5. Although preordaining the outcome of a planned meeting is not an easy task for most salespeople, it is critical if your goal is to be effective. Your objective is to say something like, "If, at the end of this meeting, you see that our service will help you to solve your problem and meet your needs, then we agree that the next step is to meet with the Financial VP to explore a timely allocation of the required funds," or "that you will visit our plant to test our product and select the right one for your application."

6. The hardest element of all is the final agreement. "If we agree during the meeting that the service my company offers is the right service for you, and if the price is amenable to both of us, then you will place the order so we can begin production. Of course, if you determine that this is not the right service at the right price then you will advise me of that and we will end our dialogue and wait until the next time you may need our services."

If you have handled the advance agreement well, then you have, in essence, closed the sale, with the parameters set for a "yes" or a "no" before you even have the meeting.

Any agreement is, by definition, a two-way street. If all the elements are agreed to verbally, then confirm them in writing. Then be sure to secure a response; an agreement has to involve both parties.

If you have a client who typically does not respond to written agreements, try this tactic that is likely to get a response to or at least an acknowledgement of your advance agreement. Write an email, fax, or letter that states the terms of the agreement and build into it a feature that will induce a response. Perhaps you can make an obvious error intentionally—one that the client will want to correct and that will move him or her to respond. For example, you can write: "We will develop a support plan for the 13 units your company owns and develop a plan for replacement as units become obsolete" although you know the firm currently has 33 units. Your client probably will want you to correct this error and will respond to your email, fax, or letter. In the process, your client also will endorse the other elements of the agreement. At a minimum, you will know that your client has read your agreement and not disagreed with it. You can always then apologize for the typo or send a correction if you do not hear from him. Again, this may serve as another enticement for the client to respond.

Another tactic to elicit a response is to add a postscript to your email, fax, or letter that has nothing to do with the agreement, but which merits an answer: "p.s.: I would like very much to invite you for a dinner. I have kept Tuesday evening open. Please confirm if this will be okay." Your prospect will have to read through the message to get to the postscript, so the response that accepts your dinner offer may include an acknowledgement of the agreement or comments about it. Even if the agreement is not acknowledged, you know the client is thinking about it; this gives you a good opening question for your meeting.

Take these steps before your next sales trip. Set up your

meeting in advance. Establish an agenda. Spell out the roles that you and your client will play, and pre-ordain the outcome of the meeting. You will save time and travel by reducing the selling cycle. The result: lower costs and the ability to close more business. You will move from 'good' to 'great'. Your company will love you, and you may even put more money in your pocket.

The Global Chameleons

All salesmen are taught that building trust is the key to successful selling. In order to build trust we try to develop a rapport with the client and, hopefully, cement a bond. Developing this relationship and the ensuing trust is a major first step to developing a long-term client.

For some companies trust is built-in. When we buy from a well-known online retailer, we trust that we will receive what we ordered and that the quality will be acceptable. There is no salesman necessary to build this trust. The brand name of the company has the trust associated with it. In addition, the value of the purchase may determine the level of trust: for example, a purchase of $19.95 requires a lower level of trust than does one of $1,995.

As salespeople, we are fortunate that most products cannot be sold directly from manufacturers to customers; the intervention of a salesperson is usually required. In international sales, especially, with all the inherent complications of differing cultures, languages, and business practices, to name a few, the role of the salesperson becomes vital. Therefore, we have to work hard to develop our rapport building capabilities in spite of these sometimes vast differences. We must be professional chameleons.

The first thing to understand is that a country's culture is made up of many elements. Some of these typically are: Language, religion, customs, and history. Being a global chameleon means trying, as much as possible, to blend into the host country and culture of a client.

It is amazing how much of a culture is transmitted through its language. Every language has three basic components–vocabulary, grammar and style of speaking. While vocabulary and grammar are necessary to speak a language, they do not convey the true 'feel' of the culture; incorporating the language's and culture's style is essential to the successful adoption of a foreign language. For example, while many people can speak other languages, they do so with their native intonation. This carries little of the culture. For even the best global chameleons, learning the language of every country you will visit is impossible, so let's jump to religion, customs, and history as better vehicles to understand the culture of a country.

There are various tools that can help us to understand the country and culture of the client we will be visiting. Certainly, books such as *Kiss, Bow or Shake Hands* by Terri Morrison and *Dun & Bradstreet's Guide to Doing Business Around the World* by Terri Morrison, Wayne A. Conaway, and Joseph J. Douress are very helpful. However, there are other books that can give us better insights into the particular country we are planning to visit. I'll mention a few of these here.

Many years ago, I was planning a trip to Saudi Arabia and Syria for a consulting project. This project put me in direct contact with local nationals of those countries and with little or no direct contact with westerners. I prepared for the trip by taking some lessons in basic Arabic so I could be as aware as possible during my communication with clients. I then bought a copy of the Koran and took time to read that book of the Muslim world. It was so fascinating that I read it a second time! This book led me find a history book of the Middle East. If you think that *The Lord of the Rings* is intriguing and exciting you will be flabbergasted by the real-life history of the Middle East. This is an unbelievably rich and intricate story full of wars, intrigues, alliances and broken alliances.

Through these readings, I began to understand the "soul" of the Arabic tribes and countries and of the Arabic world. I was by no means an expert, but at least I was not totally ignorant. I certainly had an advantage over anyone who was coming in cold.

At one point in my visit to Saudi Arabia I was invited by a wealthy sheik to a traditional Bedouin dinner with him and other associates from Arabic countries. My competitor was also invited. Because I had taken the time to learn about the culture, to speak a few words, and to adapt to the dining etiquette of the Bedouin, I was treated as guest of honor and landed the contract. I think my competitor is still trying to figure out how to stop a servant from pouring gahwa into his cup and how to eat with his right hand only.

The purpose of having this edge in knowledge is not to be able to show off, however. The knowledge will help you to understand and to ask intelligent and relevant questions, and perhaps to have an insight into the answers. In sales it is good to ask intelligent probing questions even if you think you already know the answer.

Being a good global chameleon means that when you are traveling the world, you realize that peoples are different. Try to understand those differences so you can more easily build a relationship with a client and build that relationship based on trust and respect. Due to the heavy presence of American movies, music and television shows, most other cultures have an understanding of us, no matter how erroneous they may be. On the other hand, Americans usually have little understanding of other cultures because of our isolation; we don't have a great degree of exposure to other world cultures in our country. We Americans, to be successful global chameleons, have to work at acquiring knowledge and understanding of other cultures.

The next time you travel to new lands, leave the latest novel or business bestseller at home. Instead, read about the religion, history, and culture of the countries you will visit. It will make you stand out as a salesperson and as an American.

Selling in the Product Life Cycle

Typically, products and services go through a Product Life Cycle (PLC). In the past the life cycle was typically long; with today's technological advances, a life cycle may be extremely short. Depending on where the client business is on the product life cycle curve, the selling skills of our sales force will need to be varied.

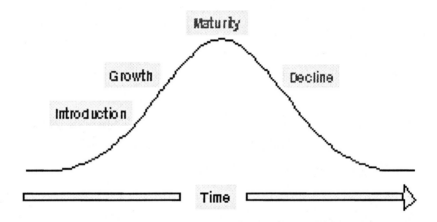

While the classic PLC is a bell curve, in reality it can have a wide variety of shapes. Over time, a product goes through four phases: Introduction, growth, maturity, and decline.

In general, there is first an Introduction Phase. This is when the product or service is unknown and the benefits have not yet been recognized.

Once the concept of the product or service is recognized and accepted we enter the Growth Phase. Unfortunately, many products never reach this phase because they have no intrinsic value or because they are not sold well. Here the market is driven by demand, and very often the supply side will lag.

This is the phase where successful products have the highest margins.

The PLC then reaches the Maturity Phase, during which most clients who need the product will have it, and the company will only need to maintain the product. This phase may be short or very, very long, as is the case with consumable products such as prescription drugs which are protected by patents.

After the Maturity Phase, the Decline Phase begins. Often the decline sets in because other companies jump in and produce competitive products, or new products come along that eclipse the current technology. After the Decline Phase, the product or service either dies or enters a phase in which it becomes a commodity. Many products and services remain in this commodity phase. In the commodity phase the profits are typically low, so costs must be kept low and economies of scale may win the day.

The types of selling at these various phases differ greatly. The success or failure of the product may depend greatly on identifying the proper selling skills and the types of salespeople required during each phase. Over the years of working with salespeople, I have identified many traits that may determine the success of a particular type of salesperson and which particular skill sets are most advantageous to have at a particular point on the PLC.

Quite often, during the Introduction Phase of a new product or service, especially in this high technology age, the product's concept may be totally unrecognized. Potential clients may be going about their business without recognizing the benefits that might be derived from the new concept. The salesperson has to have exceptional skills at leading the client to recognize the potential benefits of the new product, or, alternatively, to recognize the problems that can be avoided through use of the new product or service.

The salesperson needed here is one, first of all, who can gain access to the prospect. The prospect is not aware of the new concept, so has no 'pain' relative to it; the prospect does not feel a need or a deficiency and is, in a word, "okay". The salesperson must be able to move the prospect from feeling "okay" to the recognition that he has a problem that the new concept can fix. This "fix" may be to bring in more business, or higher margins, or reduced cost. Prospects may be completely unaware of these improvements.

My preferred approach is to use good questioning techniques to allow the prospect to recognize the potential benefits himself and get emotionally involved in the results. Sometimes a salesperson may achieve this through a features and benefits type of presentation. Often the sell is more difficult than that.

I recently worked with a company that developed a satellite-based broadband Internet portal. This is an exceptional product for remote areas that do not have the infrastructure to support broadband. This unit could be installed and service as many as 5,000 customers. Typically communications is controlled by a state agency, or by an oligopoly of a few communications companies. A salesperson must approach the powers that be in these companies and sell effectively. In this case the salesperson may sell to the decision maker using a negative approach.

After explaining the product the salesperson may ask, "I don't suppose this product would have any advantage to AllPowerful

Communications, Inc." This is a baiting question, of course. When the prospect responds in the positive, then the salesperson may ask, "How many people in this remote town might be interested in this service?" The prospect might respond that some 4,000 to 5,000 customers might be interested. "How much would each user be willing and able to pay for this?" "Perhaps $50 per month", responds the prospect. "Let's see, 5,000 users at $50 per month, how much would that be?"

Always let the prospect do the calculations. And never accept percentages. You cannot put percentages in your pocket. The benefits to be accrued must be stated by the prospect in terms of money or time or stress – something real. "Let's see…$50 times 5,000, that would be $250,000 dollars times twelve months would be three million dollars", answers the prospect. "Less the cost of the product and the service at about a million dollars, that would leave…" "About two million a year!" Now the prospect is excited. The salesman may even follow up with, "is that a decent return for a company like yours?" knowing full well that it is.

The prospect is now emotionally involved and has recognized, for himself, the value of the product. In his head he is visualizing the benefits he will derive from this product – more profits, perhaps a raise or promotion – whatever it might be. Of course, this example is oversimplified, but it does serve to illustrate the type of salesperson needed for this phase of the PLC. Connections within the industry should be strong in order to be able to get to the decision makers. The powers of influence and persuasion must be superb. Anything short of this could spell disaster.

Often, these new products are developed by entrepreneurs. These entrepreneurs often lack basic selling skills. Yet they insist on selling the product themselves, because they understand the product best. This is very often a recipe for failure. Find a great salesperson with exceptional skills and pay the piper. Your future may depend on it.

The next phase, hopefully, is the Growth Phase. The demand is strong. Competition is weak or nonexistent. This is the phase we salespeople love because we can sit back and enjoy watching our work from the previous phase pay off. But what types of salespeople are needed during the Growth Phase? It could be that we do not need salespeople at all. Perhaps all we need are order-takers; these people often think of themselves as salespeople, but they really require minimal sales skills.

So what should be done with the salesperson who got you here during the Introduction Phase? Oftentimes, promoting this person to a management position is a mistake. The skills needed to launch a new product are not the same as those required to be an effective manager, even though a person could have both sets of skills. Hold onto this person and find her some new challenges. She may come in very handy in a later phase.

The Maturity Phase is also very nice to experience. Once you enter this phase, you have saturated the market and are selling replacements or expendable items to go with the product. Costs are low and cash flow is good. Customer service takes over from sales. But keep that startup salesperson around. Her time is approaching.

Some time after the Maturity Phase comes the Decline Phase. Decline may come about for a variety of reasons. Perhaps competitors have caught on and are offering knock-off products or services. Perhaps a new technology has come along that will antiquate yours. The decline also may be gradual, or it may be precipitous.

As an aside, I spent almost 10 years in the Army. I went through Basic Training three times—once as a recruit, once as an officer candidate, and again as a junior officer. At least 99% of the training in the Army is how to "take the hill", how to advance. Virtually no time is spent on how to keep your butt intact when you are in retreat or being overrun. The same is true of the typical MBA program. Every class focuses on how to be successful, ignoring the fact that totally different skills and knowledge are required to keep from falling into a black hole and how to keep your butt intact while experiencing a debilitating decline.

Hopefully you kept your top-notch salesperson from the Introduction Phase around, because now is the time to bring her back into the fray. These will be tough times, potentially with layoffs and cost reductions. Hopefully you will have other products at various positions in the PLC so you can shift resources. One helpful resource shift is to get the salesperson involved in slowing the decline. It will take powerful selling skills to keep customers, get ideas from them, and perhaps find ways to lengthen and mitigate the decline. Great questioning skills and a very strong constitution are required. The order takers will not cut it here. They will get scared and bail out for greener pastures. Only a seasoned salesperson who loves challenges will survive and be of help.

You will have to recognize what the goal of this phase is. You cannot turn back the clock. The objective is to continue to prosper after the decline. You will then hopefully enter the final phase which is the commodity phase. Your product or service is now a commodity. There are many suppliers of the same or similar products. The differentiators between you and the competitors are weak or non-existent. You have to rely on efficiencies of scale and a different selling approach.

The salespeople you need now do not have the same skills as the introducer or the order takers. You now are in need of relationship builders. The differentiator between your company and the competitors will be your salespeople. Your name and reputation may carry some weight, but the bulk of the difference will be your sales force.

Most of the salespeople in the world fit into this category. It is rare to have the chance to introduce a new concept, and it is not new for long. Once it is a commodity different skills and behaviors are required. Trust must be built. Maintaining the customer relationship is paramount. Taking customers away from competitors is the only way to grow. Increase the market share, and the increase can only come from the competitor's pocket.

Just because we are in a commodity market does not mean that selling is easy. And there will be great salespeople and there will be washouts. Most will be mediocre. Find and develop the great ones. You want salesmen with good people skills, the ability to build trust and confidence with clients and prospects. They also have to be good hunters, always looking for openings to take a customer away from a competitor.

Last week I did sales training for a group of private bankers. This is a typical commodity service. In this industry, there are lots of competitors and little differentiation among them. The bankers needed to develop good questioning skills to detect what problems their prospects were having, and then learn how to determine the effects of these problems. They needed strong business development skills, including how to get referrals and networking.

These are all typical skills of salespeople who are successful in the commodity phase. The product could be farm equipment or spare parts, computer, legal or consulting services. You can imagine how many products and services fall into this category. Perhaps yours!

Meanwhile, what has happened to the super startup salesperson? Unless you have found a way to challenge her in your company, she has probably started her own company and is ready to compete with you in the near future.

Non-Productive Time Wasters

Being a global salesman is fun and rewarding. We get to travel around the world, eat in great restaurants, put together mega-deals and meet some of the most fascinating people. On that wonderful event, the international business trip, we work from breakfast to late at night, being creative and solving client problems. We come home from these often long trips with a sense of excitement and accomplishment.

Then we get back to the office and back to the routine. The first few days back are still great. We are following up on the wonderful events of our trip, resuming relationships with family and friends. Hopefully we have a good support person to bring into the loop, and hard-working people in other departments to whom you can pass the baton. They can pick up the various opportunities that you were able to develop and run with them.

After a few days or a week the trip seems years away. Perhaps the next trip is still a few weeks, or months away. Now is the real challenge: how to remain productive while you spend time at the home office. I have wasted a lot of valuable time in my life when I was in this mode. Here are five of the worst non-productive time stealers. Be careful to avoid them and stay on the right side of the productivity line.

1. Working with the clock instead of with your daily goals. You are in sales. You do not get paid by the hour. You get paid and you get ahead based on your achievements. Forget the clock. Set your goals for the day — goals that are based on what you want to accomplish

in the longer term. If you work against the clock you will spend more time playing computer solitaire that being productive. When you achieve your daily goals, go play golf or read a book.

2. Making long socializing phone calls to clients and non-clients. Your telephone calls should have a point and a purpose. If you just want to keep in contact with existing clients try to find something productive to call about. Getting a referral is always a good bet. You can wile away the hours chatting about sports or fun times, but you may be interrupting a potential client's valuable production time.

3. Pushing papers. Some of us become experts at this. We can work on long-range business plans, re-analyze our budget, and move papers from one stack to another. All of these consume large amounts of time, but produce no sales. Get these projects out of the way quickly and move on to income-producing activities.

4. Writing proposals and assembling literature packets, when we do not know the next step. A few years ago, I took a job as President of a consulting company owned by a very large French bank. We did business development consulting for European companies wanting to enter the U. S. through acquisition, partnerships or creation of distribution networks. We wanted to expand the customer base by assisting U.S. companies in developing business in Europe.

Like most salesmen, I became really excited when a company expressed interest in using our services and requested a proposal. I would rush back into my office in Manhattan and spend three days working on a proposal, involving others in the office and in our offices in Europe—a large time and effort commitment.

Once I finished the beautiful proposal I sent it to the prospect for consideration. Then would begin the eternal sales game of following up. I left message after message but receive no call back. I could not understand. They were really excited when I had visited with them.

One day I met a friend who had been in the consulting business much longer than I had. He laughed when I lamented to him about my situation. He said, mocking me "Vince, don't you know that the best way to get rid of a salesman is to feign interest and ask for a proposal. You have to make sure you know what is going to happen next before you send a proposal." You cannot imagine how much wasted time I have saved since I learned this timely and valuable lesson.

5. Getting ready to get ready. This time waster might include: studying product specifications beyond what is required, working on your computer, surfing the Internet, putting together a newsletter, and sitting at your desk, staring into space, waiting for a client to call. While all of these activities (except the last), are necessary to some degree, if taken to the extreme they become the perfect non-productive time wasters. I am

sure you can list many more, including your own particular bugaboos.

The key to being productive as a global salesperson is not to be constantly in the sales development role, but to achieve a balance between work that brings in revenue and work that is in a supporting role. Be very careful not to let the balance get out of whack. Time is your most valuable commodity in sales, and we cannot afford to waste it.

I watched President Bush's "State of the Union" address last week. After his speech, the Democrats were given equal time, in a feigned attempt at fairness. In a similar attempt, the next part of this chapter will look at what you CAN do to improve sales productivity in between trips.

Using Your Back-Home Time Productively

The following are five areas on which you should concentrate to gain the most value from your time:

1. First, you should spend time disqualifying all the "suspects" you met on your business trips. Only a relatively small percentage of the prospects you met while traveling will be worthwhile to continue chasing. These are the "prospects". Many of the contacts you made are "suspects", who are, likely, not worthy of you spending your valuable time. One of the most important and least understood aspects of selling is disqualifying the suspects as quickly as possible, so that you can spend quality time with true prospects and clients.

   This concept requires a total change in mindset. That is, instead of having a "full pipeline", you want to be cleaning out that pipeline as quickly and efficiently as possible. You do not have the time to waste talking to "suspects" who are unlikely to give you enough business to justify your time spent. You want to work hard to disqualify anyone who is not worth your effort.

There can be many reasons to disqualify a prospect. You will need excellent questioning techniques to be able to accomplish this in an expedient manner. Most of the time you will disqualify prospects because he does not have a problem or need that you can solve. Refer him to someone who can solve his problem, and get a referral. You may disqualify the prospect because the budget or volume of business is not sufficient. The decision process that the prospect uses may not be acceptable to you. The most extreme case of the disqualifying process requires fighting to get the prospect to say "No!" to you. These are prospects who you no longer want for a client. When you meet these people, you will sometimes have to fight for them to say "NO!"

After you disqualify the "suspects", do spend time cultivating the true prospects and your existing clients.

2. The second thing you should do is network. We are blessed in an international city like Miami to have a large number of bi-lateral chambers of commerce. Attend these meetings and judge their value. Zero in on a couple of chambers that can be most useful to you, and get involved in them. Take a look at other organizations you may wish to join for networking pur-

poses. While Rotary in the U.S. is primarily comprised of fairly small business people, in other countries it is a very prestigious organization with high-powered members. Look into organizations such as this to advance your prospecting possibilities.

There are two types of networking in which you should be involved. One is aimed at providing prospects for your company, and the other is aimed at providing exposure for yourself. Industry trade shows and professional associations will allow you to promote yourself. This provides a perfect segue to the third item on my list.

3. Get exposure for yourself and your company by writing professional articles and doing free talks. I am always amazed at how few people, people with in-depth knowledge of their industries and markets, write articles for publication in trade journals and make speeches about their industry, markets or company. Make a concerted effort to get noticed and bring attention to your company. You will be recognized as a very special person if you can get published and invited as a public speaker.

4. I guess I am biased because I am in the education business, but I believe that you are never finished learning. Take time to continue your education. This can be trade education, professional education or an advanced degree. The world changes very quickly. You cannot keep your head buried in the past and rely on what you learned before. Enroll in

classes, attend workshops and keep furthering your education.

5. And the fifth element to being productive is to always remember that salespeople are never successful by being on "clock" time. The clock is your enemy. Set your goals! Concentrate on short-term behavioral goals that will lead you to both short-term and long-term success. Create a "recipe" for success and reduce it to the lowest common denominator – the day, week or month. And then stay on you "goal" time. Insure that you achieve your daily goals every single day. Forget the clock; achieve your goals.

Include in these goals all the ingredients you need to be successful. The mix is different for each person. It may include cold calling, follow-ups with existing clients, networking, direct mail or email, writing articles or arranging speaking engagements, and many other items. Think this through and then develop a daily, weekly and monthly recipe and stick with it. Your boss may not understand, but, when you have completed your goals for the day, week, or month, play golf!

Vincent S. Daniels

Questions Bring More Than Answers

Every person involved in sales knows that asking the right questions is the key to successful selling. Unfortunately, whenever I do sales training, I see that most salespeople, although they know this, have very little idea of how to really ask the right questions. Many do not even know the real reasons for asking questions. In *Spin Selling*, Neil Rackham covers a lot about questioning, and what we should try to achieve through questioning, but he does not specifically address the *techniques* salespeople need to develop as *skills* in order to be successful.

Some of the techniques that I teach in seminars I learned while serving in the U. S. Army. I had the good fortune to go through Military Intelligence (sometimes referred to as an oxymoron) school in Fort Holabird, Maryland. In this spy training academy we learned interviewing and interrogating techniques. Many of these same techniques can be used in sales. Of course, thumb screws and the rack are out. But most of the rest is very applicable. The other techniques presented in this article were learned in life and in sales training.

After seeing this over and over as a major impediment to success in selling, I developed a tool to assist in learning and perfecting questioning techniques. The tool I use in training I call the BIRD DOG Questioning Techniques®. Of course, each one of the letters means something. But before we get into the techniques let us define "question" as it pertains to sales (and spying). A question is something designed to evoke a response or information from the client or prospect. A statement such as "Please tell me more" will qualify as a question. The desired response can be an answer, a physical reaction, a heightening of emotion, or even silence. Even the "question" itself could be no more than a facial expression, gesture, sound or, as above, even silence.

I realize that this is complex (and your seventh grade teacher would never agree), but we are grown salespeople now and we must understand the tools of our trade. And our trade is to gather and evaluate information, get the client emotionally involved, and make a sale. All "questions" must lead to these ends.

One reason that we must become experts in the art of questioning is that often the client does not know what the real problem is. Just like a psychiatrist we must assist the client or prospect to realize what the real problem is. We are the experts and we need information from the client in order to guide him and us to the root of the problem. We also want the client to "feel" the problem as we progress. As discovered by Neil Rackham, we want the client to realize and acknowledge the effect of the problem. We use questioning techniques to dig out the effects of the problem, and to get the client to feel them.

Many times the client does not even realize she has a problem. In these days of "ever-improving" (debatable) technology, this is often the case. For example, I just had a salesman in to help me to re-wire my stereo system. I am very proud of my stereo. I bought all the best components. His suggestion was to junk it. Technology has made it obsolete. I did not know I had a problem, but now I am going to invest a bucket of money to not only update, but radically change the way I store and listen to music. I did not know that I had a problem, but the salesman helped me to realize this, and to then offer a solution. He did not offer a solution early. He found out all the information he needed first, and then got me emotionally involved by discovering my love affair with high-end equipment and good music quality and appealing to it. Only then did he offer a solution. I was already sold.

Through our questioning technique we have to lead our prospect through a journey. This journey may be described in many ways, but the destination is always the same: disqualify the prospect or make the sale.

One approach is to begin with asking the question: What is the problem? We want the client to discover or admit to what the problem is. We then lead the prospect to understand and verbalize "why" it is a problem, and to explore the effects of the problem on his life or business. Often, or even usually, the client has not yet analyzed the effects of the problem. The salesman, as doctor or psychiatrist, must help the client to realize the impact or effects of the problem. Only then can he become emotionally involved, and begin to "feel" his pain or pleasure. I'll say more about this medical analogy in a little while.

Another way to think of the selling journey is that prospects usually like to remain in the "intellectual" area. They do not want to get emotionally involved with the problem, especially while a salesman is present. Our job is to get them from the intellectual statement of a problem to a "personal" involvement and recognition of the problem. We use good questioning techniques to help the prospect to cross this very difficult threshold. We want them personally involved in the problem. This journey is compounded by the fact that the salesman herself is afraid of entering the emotionally charged personal area. The salesperson will very often retreat to the safe intellectual ground, even when a personal involvement is revealed by the client. This goes back to one of our childhood rules from mother – don't ask personal questions. We have to get over this script that is imbedded in our psyche in order to be effective salespeople or managers. (Other scripts we must rid ourselves of are "Don't ask about money!" and " Don't talk to strangers.")

Once we have the client personally involved in the problem, it is fairly easy to get the prospect emotionally involved. This is where we want to arrive in order to make the sale. The emotional involvement may be about the product, the problem, the solution or even liking and trusting the salesperson.

Another way to look at the journey, especially with new products or concepts is the medical approach. When you arrive on the sales call the client is in good health. She does not even know that she has a problem. The salespersons' job is to move the prospect from feeling well to feeling not-so-well—to discover and admit their pain. "Perhaps the way we have been doing it is not the best way." The old adage "Don't fix it if it ain't broke" does not work so well in this age of ever-changing technology, and of bureaucracies that continue to propagate and eventually die under their own weight. This is an age of remaining competitive through constantly *considering* change.

Once we have the prospect feeling not-so-well, we can move on to helping the prospect feel downright sick, and perhaps even critical. Getting the client to consider the effects of the problem, or of not making the change, can usually achieve this end.

BIRD DOG Questioning Techniques ®

We all know that questions are very important to selling. As discussed previously, "questions" in sales are not the same as grammatical "questions". In sales, we define a question as anything that gets a response from a prospect or client. (I often use the terms prospect and client interchangeably, as a client is almost always a prospect for an additional product or service.) The response from the client may be verbal or emotional, an answer, another question or a feeling that we wish to instill, such as excitement, pain, pleasure, guilt, etc. In order to understand questions, and to be able to use them effectively, we have to categorize them by the type of question, or by what we want to achieve through the question. I have developed a memory tool to help salespeople to understand the classification of questions, the BIRD DOG Questioning Techniques.

The "B" in BIRD DOG stands for several categories that usually initiate a sales visit: beginning, business, and bonding. The beginning and business questions are used to break the ice and to learn something about the client's business. Hopefully, the salesman has taken some time in advance to learn about the prospect's company and can use this information to ask good questions. These questions can also include bonding questions. These can be used to re-establish bonds set at earlier meetings. "How is your daughter doing in law school?" would be typical of this type of question. Be relatively certain that she is doing great and did not get kicked out before you ask the question, of course. It could backfire on you.

The beginning questions will usually revolve around size and scope of the business, trends, etcetera. We hope that through these beginning questions we can develop a relationship with the client and learn details about the business.

I always tell salesmen, especially on a first visit: Do not go on a sales call, but rather as an interview; interview is the "I" in BIRD DOG. On this interview, we want to establish whether or not the prospect is a viable candidate to be a client. We have to qualify or disqualify them based on this interview. Interviewing questions are designed to get the prospect telling us about her problems, and to get emotionally involved in the selling process. We should also use interviewing questions to get the client talking to us and to make sure that the conversation stays on track.

To understand which kinds of questions are used in interviewing, just tune in to Barbara Walters or Diane Sawyer. They and other television interviewers are the experts. Also, watch the tv cop shows and study their interrogating techniques.

A typical interviewing question is of the "Tell me more" variety. But quite often the interviewing questions are simple conjunctions followed by silence. You will see the interviewers making great use of conjunctions such as "And......." or "So......" followed by silence to be filled in by the subject of the interview. Sometimes just silence is a very effective interviewing technique. We are usually very reluctant to use silence as a questioning technique. We as salespeople always want to jump in and rescue the client if he seems to be struggling with an answer. We have to overcome this problem. We need to allow people time to think. This is especially true of clients who are professionals such as engineers or architects; they often have to go completely through a problem in their heads before they can respond. We have to give them this time, or we are defeating ourselves by not letting them internalize and feel the potential problem.

In the western world, silence is scary. We always try to jump in and fill the void. In sales learn to control this tendency. You will find that silence can be a great questioning technique.

So we have interviewed and it appears that we have a prospect sitting in front of us. She may actually start asking us questions. That is the best thing that can happen in sales, because now we have the opportunity to use the "R" in BIRD DOG: reverse.

When I teach sales, I am always amazed that 95 percent of salespeople have no idea of what reversing is and how to do it. Reversing is based on a simple premise. Every time a client asks a question, she has a reason. It is the duty of the salesperson to find out the reason. Finding out the reason for the question will lead directly to the client's pain—in other words, the client's motivation. Pay attention here, because the client will not admit his pain right away. To find out what is motivating a prospect, a salesperson must become an expert at reversing.

If a prospect asks, "What is your company's record on on-time delivery?", he is asking for a reason. Perhaps he has had problems with his current supplier. Perhaps late deliveries have cost him in lost production. The actual question is very intellectual, but the reason behind the question may be loaded with emotion. Maybe he is going to lose his job if he cannot find a supplier who can deliver as promised. If the salesperson just answers the question he has missed a major opportunity to find out what is motivating the buyer and to find out what kinds of problems are plaguing him.

Often, there is not even a question that has to be reversed, but rather a statement or situation. The prospect may say, "I have heard that you guys are usually on-time with deliveries." That is not a question; it is a statement. However, underlying it is a concern. The salesperson has the duty to reverse to find out why the client made this statement. A client never asks pointless questions or makes pointless statements. There is always a reason. Find out what the reason is.

Even a situation can be reversed. If a prospect agrees to invite you in for a meeting she has a reason. Time is valuable! Unless you are gorgeous there is probably a strong business reason for spending time with you. You have to find out what the reason is.

Okay, so now we understand why we have to use the reverse. But how do we do it. It is really very simple, but is very difficult to do well. When a prospect asks a question we have to respond with another question. Generally the question we respond with is "There must be a reason you asked me that", followed by silence. You can mutate the question, but do not get too fancy. We want to find out the reason why the question was asked. Another possibility is that we ask what the client meant by the question. "When you say delivery is important, what do you mean?" Once again looking for the reason.

It is interesting that when I teach reversing, and explain it fully, students still fail to ask the right question. They get too fancy and miss the point of the reverse. It is to discover the reason for the question or statement. Keep it simple.

Also, many salespeople feel that it is too "in your face" to not answer the question and reverse it instead. Indeed, reversing can come across in this way. To make the reverse more palatable we preface it with a softening statement. This can be something like "That's a good question.", or "I'm glad you asked.", and then follow with the reverse. To be good at reversing is a skill and requires lots of practice. But superiority in sales reversing must be mastered.

The most effective reverse is where the salesman does not answer the question, but, instead, performs an effective reverse. The reason for not answering the question is that you may give the wrong answer. The answer may alienate the customer. It is best to find out why they are asking before offering up an answer.

Another option, until good reversing skills are developed, is to answer the question, and then reverse. "Yes, we are known for having the best deliveries in the business, but there must be a reason you asked me that". Remember that as a salesperson you have a right to ask a question whenever you answer a question. You not only have a right, you have a duty to yourself, to your company, and to your client.

The next type of question in the BIRD DOG Questioning Techniques is the "D", the dumb question. This does not mean that you want to appear to be stupid, although that is a valid tactic in negotiating. This means that you use your knowledge to ask good questions, instead of showing it off by talking all the time. It also means asking questions even when you think you know the answer.

Sometimes professionals, such as engineers and lawyers, feel that they have to exhibit all their knowledge in order to convince prospective clients that they know what they are talking about. In fact, what they have to do is use their knowledge to ask the right questions. Let the client fill in the answer. When the client answers the question he becomes emotionally or personally involved while giving the answer. If you can learn how to use your knowledge to ask "Dumb" questions you will see your selling success rise to a new level.

The use of dumb questions is especially important when you think you know the answer. The only person who really knows what the problem is, although she may not fully recognize it, is the client. You have to get the client talking about the problem. Using a dumb question like, "I'm confused, could you please explain why…?" We want to find out what is going to motivate the client to make a decision.

Normally, when a prospect repeats an answer he delves more deeply into the problem. Sometimes we use dumb questions just to get the client more personally involved in the answer. We may say "I'm not sure I understand.", even if we feel we do understand.

Those of you more seasoned television watchers will remember the "Colombo" series. This detective was the master of the dumb question, and he usually roped in the suspect and let him hang himself through the use of dumb questions. He would say something like, "Excuse me, I'm not sure I understand.", even though really did. A la Colombo, we could say "Let me see if I have this straight," and make an error on purpose. Or ask the prospect to repeat the answer so you can make notes.

Always remember that the dumb question is predicated on having knowledge and understanding. You are not showing that you are stupid, only that you need clarification. "A while ago you said *blank.*, and I'm not exactly sure what you meant.", or "I read in the paper that your company is going to *blank*. I was wondering: what kinds of benefits do you anticipate from this move?"

The second letter "D" in BIRD DOG stands for digging. This is not so much a technique as a strategy. In *Spin Selling*, Neil Rackham wrote that what separates the good salespeople from the great is the ability to find out the effect of the problem on the company, or on the person involved. Only approximately 20% of salespeople develop the skills and courage to tackle this question.

Once we uncovered a problem through interviewing we moved to the personalization of the problem in order to get the client emotionally involved. We will enhance the emotional involvement and peel away the intellectual denial if we get the client to discuss, and thereby realize, the effect that the problem is having on her and her company.

We may continue to use interviewing, reversing, and dumb questions during the digging process. Dumb questions can help to increase the intensity of the pain the client is feeling. But first we have to get the prospect to open up and tell us the effect or effects the problem is causing. These effects can be monetary, emotional, or involve loss of an intangible, such as time. We as salespeople do not know what the possible effects are, but we can help the client to realize them through the use of good questioning techniques.

A good tactic to find effect is to use the third party, multiple choice question. "I have seen this problem before with clients. Usually when someone has this problem it leads to lost revenue, lower productivity and even key employees leaving. I don't suppose it has any effects like that on your company."

The effect may be on the company, but the personal effect may be an even stronger motivator. Might he lose his job? Is she having sleepless nights, tension, and anxiety? Is too much time wasted on non-productive activities?

But don't stop there. Dig for the effect. Help the client to recognize and feel the effect. If you can do this you will begin to enter the arena of the great salespeople. And always remember that effects are in emotions, money, or time. They are never in percentages.

I once had a prospect tell me that he could realize a 10 – 15% increase in revenue if he could improve sales by just two or three percent. I asked what his sales were at the time. I then played dumb, "Let's see, what would 15% of that be?" I did not calculate it; I let him find a calculator and do the math. He came up with a figure of nearly $2 million. I then followed with another dumb question. "Is that a lot of money for a company as large as yours?" Two million is always a lot of money. I sold the sales training without ever having to present. Remember, you cannot put percentages in your pocket.

Next we encounter what most salespeople dread, the "O" in BIRD DOG: Objections. I once read somewhere that an objection should be very welcome, because it shows that the client is interested. That is often true, but the footnote to that statement is that the objection has only two possible outcomes—it kills the deal, or it can be overcome. If it kills the deal, that is okay because you do not have to waste any more time. You can come back to fight another day on another deal. But work hard to be absolutely sure that the objection cannot be overcome. This will often take great effort and ingenuity.

A problem with objections is that, except in the simplest circumstances and with the most talented salesperson, the salesperson cannot overcome the objection. Only the client can do that. Our job, once again, is to help the client to overcome the objection. You can probably guess what technique we will use. Right! Questions!

What is an objection? It is a roadblock imposed by the client that can either derail or stall the decision. Some objections are real, while many are contrived. In negotiating we talk about "position versus interest". Often, a client will throw out an objection to one element of the sale, when he really wants to affect another. A prospect can take a position which is very different from his real objective. We, as salespeople, have to find out whether the objection is real or contrived by the client in order to get some other concession.

Some objections are automatic; these are objections that are scripted into our behavior. One of the most common objections is price. "That's expensive!" objects the prospect, often not having any idea as to whether it is expensive or not. Mama just always said "That's expensive!" whenever a price was given. This is called the "flinch move" in negotiating.

I encountered a memorable objection of this kind while training a group of dentists in sales. Here is the story I heard from them at the beginning of sales training. When the dentist would tell his prospective client that a near-perfect smile would cost approximately $14,000, the response was nearly automatic. "That's expensive!" Then, the dentist would traditionally start to explain why it cost so much, and then start lowering the price. I taught the dentists just two words to use in this scenario: "Which means?" The patient almost never knows what she means when she blurts out, "That's expensive!" It is just a conditioned response. When you ask the question, "What do you mean when you say expensive?" the argument will normally just wilt away. The patients had not gone shopping around for the best price. They came to a dentist they trust. Stand by your price, as long as it is fair, and add to your bottom line.

So how do you overcome objections? Earlier I mentioned that it requires ingenuity; and when it comes to ingenuity, the saying "two heads work better than one" holds true. In this case, one mind with an idea feeds on the other. So bring the client into the problem-solving process. Ask a good question. "We have a problem. Any ideas?", or, "If you were me what would you do?" The one I like the best, but never had the courage to use is, "Let's talk about this. You start."

In short, you want to discover whether the problem is real or contrived, then you want to let the client show you how the problem can be overcome. If the two of you can honestly not come up with a solution, then the sale is over. Move on.

Another problem with objections is that prospects usually wait until late in the selling cycle to offer them up. Clients feel that the objection has much more power if it comes late in the process, after you have invested a lot of time and effort. They are right. The 80/20 rule is in effect. 80% of concessions are given up in the last 20% of the negotiation. So how can we combat this?

Once again you can use your knowledge and experience to your advantage. If you know that with this type of prospect, invariably a certain objection comes up, or if you can sense that a particular objection will come up, then be the first to bring it up. And bring it up early. For example, "Sometimes when I visit a large company like yours the small size of my company can be a problem. Do you foresee this as a problem?"

I know that this tactic is quite scary for most salesmen to contemplate, but think about it for a moment. Do you prefer that an objection be taken care of early in the process, or after you have invested time and effort? If the objection is going to be a deal-killer, when would you like to know? Get the objections that you can foresee on the table early.

In the mid-90s, I was being interviewed for a high-level job as President of a company in New York. The company was the consulting arm of a major French bank. I passed the first rounds of interviews, and then the senior person at the bank and the president of the consulting company in Europe flew in to interview me—on the Concorde. I was the last of three candidates to be interviewed. After we went through the niceties (Beginning questions) they were ready to enter phase two in which they ask questions. Instead, I jumped to phase three, during which I am supposed to ask questions. I foresaw two possible objections and wanted them to be on the table early.

I asked the two executives: "I am very interested in this position, but I envision two problems that you might have. First, I don't speak very much French, and, secondly, my experience in consulting is fairly limited. Are these issues going to eliminate me from consideration?

I did have extensive experience in management, and I knew that that was the strength that they were interested in, but I wanted to know if these other issues would kill the deal. They left the room for a few minutes to confer. When they returned they advised that these shortcomings would not be a problem. The interview continued and I was offered the job. I later met the other candidates, and they both spoke fluent French and had extensive consulting experience. I believe that bringing up these obstacles myself, early in the interview, closed the deal. This illustrates the power of overcoming obstacles early in the game.

Finally, the "G" in BIRD DOG stands for "getting the decision". This sometimes requires the ultimate selling technique, "Going for No!"

For most of us, if we have followed a sound selling process, asked the right questions and, perhaps, provided a good presentation, getting the decision is quite easy. We just ask for the business. I usually ask "What do you want to do now?", or "What is the next step?" You can use hundreds of contrived closing techniques, and you can buy many books about them. These may be good for one-call closers and store clerks, but when dealing with sophisticated buyers on an international playing field, these are likely to turn people away rather than towards the sale. According to studies done by Target Training International, Ltd (TTI). The top salespeople in the United States are hard drivers, described as Persuaders, followed by Promoters and Conductors. For those of you familiar with the DISC profile used by TTI, these would be high "D" and high "I". In Germany, on the other hand, the top salespeople are very high Promoters (high "I"), followed by Relaters and Supporters (High "S"). This indicates that while the U.S. top salespeople are pretty direct closers, the Germans tend more toward relationship building and influencing decisions. This is probably indicative of the culture and the expectations of the clients. The top U.S. salesperson who is a "closer" may alienate a German client, while the U.S. client may think that the top German salesperson is very slow to get to the point.

Therefore, how you close the sale, or develop the client relationship before you go for the decision will definitely be affected by the culture of the region. It may be quite different in New York than in rural Alabama.

There is, in my opinion, one commonality among top salespeople: They understand that, at some point, you have to get a "No!" from a prospect! There is some point where you have to force a decision. The best salespeople recognize this point and force the question early. Bad salespeople might allow the sales course to continue for much too long because they are afraid of getting a "No!" from the customer, and are even more afraid of fighting to get one.

Going for a "No!" is not an easy task. First we must try to get a yes. We must use all our selling abilities to get that yes. Once those avenues are exhausted we go for a "No!'.

The easiest way to go for that "No!" is to ask questions from a negative standpoint, assuming a "No!". I used this in one case when trying to sign up a new distributor in Brazil for some expendable products. Being a distributor required a starting inventory of $100,000 in order to properly service the market. I had tried to get a "Yes!" but they were evading the decision. The evasion was not because they were not convinced, but just a delaying tactic that was probably part of their psyche. Mama told them to never make decisions on the spot. But I needed a decision because I had to return home and it is much more difficult to get a decision over the phone or through email than it is in person.

I pulled out negative questioning techniques out of my selling skills toolkit and gave them a try. I had nothing to lose, as the client was at an impasse. I asked, "It seems you are interested in this product line, but you are probably not ready to make an initial order right now." I presumed the negative. I was taking the candy away from them. They responded that, no they were very interested in moving forward. Still not a yes or no!

I pulled out my second negative question, "But you are probably not ready to place an initial order." They knew the required amount, so I did not repeat that, and that omission came back to haunt me in the final negotiation, but that is another story. The good news is that, after the partners looked at one another, they caved in and said yes, they wanted to place the initial order, so I pulled out a recommended inventory list and we started working on it.

Sometimes you have to use much stronger tactics in going for the "No!" When a prospect stays neutral, wanting to think it over, you may have to fight hard for that "No!" In the case of selecting a distributor, for example, you may be talking with your first choice. Your second choice may be waiting for your visit while you are still in-country. You want to leave with one distributor signed, so you need an absolute, a yes or no, and not a stall. The prospect may be using the stall as a strategic tactic to keep you from signing on with his competitor. You need that "No!"

If the situation gets this critical, which is rarely the case, I use another negative tactic. "Usually when someone tells me they want to think it over they really mean no. Maybe they are afraid of hurting my feelings by telling me no. Does your indecision really mean "No?" I have to take it that you really mean

"No!" It is okay. I understand that our product is not right for everyone".

Do not rescue them. Shut your mouth and let them wrestle with the answer. You have just closed the book and taken away the candy. Prospects hate to be told "No!" But you want a no or a yes so you can move along. Force the issue, get a "No!", or say "No!" to them.

Now, many salespeople feel that the first "No!" is where the selling begins. It is true that many "No!" statements can be turned into a "Yes!" by a good salesman. Once again, use all your skills. But the final "No!" is not a bad thing either. What we do not want to do is to lose time or another opportunity. A "No!" will give us the freedom to move along and not waste time beating that dead horse. Sometimes we will make a mistake and lose a sale. But on the whole we will gain by having more time to be productive and spend with customers who are less challenging.

Going for "No!" takes courage and resolve. Most salespeople have to move slowly into this tactic. We have lots of scripting and comfort zone issues to confront. But if, step by step, you can become stronger at going for "No!", you will move into the top ranks of sales.

That is the story of the BIRD DOG Questioning Techniques®. Develop these special skills and see your productivity soar.

Vincent S. Daniels

Help from the Government

I remember a joke among entrepreneurs some years ago. What are the worst words for an entrepreneur to hear? "We are from the government and we are here to help."

While most of the time government help translates into government meddling, there is one exception. This exception means that help, and generally good help reasonably priced, is available to the global sales person. It comes from the U.S. Commercial Service and its Export Assistance Centers.

I have taken advantage of these services for many years, usually with good results: I have taken part in trade missions and trade shows, used the international partner search and made good use of the Gold Key service.

There are some obvious advantages to having the U.S. Commercial Service as your partner in developing new international business. The cachet attached to the name carries a lot of weight in any country in the world. When someone from the U.S. Commercial Service (USCS) calls to set up an appointment for you the gatekeepers cannot resist, and it saves you many international calls, many emails and lots of frustration.

Of all the services available the Gold Key is the most useful. Basically, you have all the resources of the U.S. Department of Commerce working to set up meaningful appointments for you in a new market. You will have to work with your Export Assistant to insure that all the parameters of your target audience are understood, but usually most of the appointments are of good value. You have to remember that the people working for you in-country are local nationals, and they may not be extremely knowledgeable about your industry. You must help them. And some companies will sneak themselves into your appointment calendar even though their real motive is to sell you something.

I have used the Golden Key service in Caracas, Santiago and Belo Horizonte, to help set up meetings with end users and potential distributors. The services went very well, and I even had service beyond the call of duty in both cases. In Belo Horizonte the Commercial Assistant drove me around and went with me on my visits. This was a great assistance, even though I spoke reasonable Portuguese. His presence opened many doors and added a personal touch to the service. I believe it was also very valuable to him, as he saw what was expected of a Gold Key user and how local companies responded to the visit.

In Caracas I was supplied with a translator as part of the package, although my Spanish is also okay. The translator was helpful in many ways, especially in recommending good restaurants for new client meetings; we even sampled a couple.

The Golden Key service is very reasonable. The cost ranges between $250 and $800 a day, depending on destination. Of course, the quality of the service depends entirely on the interest and abilities of the local USCS assistance. Some are better than others. If the local Commercial Assistants are not properly supervised you may end up meeting lots of relatives and friends who are "in the business". Nepotism is, unfortunately, not dead.

Also, the level of research available through the USCS will vary greatly. When I used the International Partner Search in a number of countries to find suitable distributors the results were mixed. Some did a good job, while others, I think, just used the yellow pages. You have to work closely with your International Trade Specialist to insure that you get the best service.

In one extreme case, many years ago, I was referred to three possible distributors. When I tried to contact them I found that two were already out of business, and the other represented my main competitor. Need I repeat, work closely with your USCS International Trade Specialist to avoid these potential pitfalls.

Beyond the Gold Key and International Partner Search, the USCS offers International Market Research, Customized Market Analysis, International Company Profile and Trade Shows and Missions.

The trade shows I attended were well run and promoted. The trade mission I attended (Portugal, Spain, Turkey and Greece) was excellent. I met many future clients, agents, and members with whom I later collaborated on business deals for many years. A double-edged benefit!

As an international businessman I used to lament the fact that many countries did much more to support their exporters, from paying for attendance at major trade shows to allowing bribes to be legally written off. It seemed that Americans were always at a disadvantage. With the support of the USCS we can at least reduce that level of disadvantage greatly. And the fee we pay for the service, in a laissez-faire economy, means that the anti-commerce representatives in our government cannot point fingers at "government support of businesses", even though, in the words of President Calvin Coolidge, "the business of the United States is business."

For more information on government assistance to exporters visit the website www.export.gov. There you will find links to the United States Commercial Service offices. Here in Florida the Florida District Export Council has set up a website with valuable links and information, www.floridaexporter.com. The Local USCS office will have, at their beck and call 157 USCS offices in 84 countries, as well as 105 Export Assistance Centers in the United States, all there to help promote U.S. companies and products.

Ethics in Global Sales – An Oxymoron?

In 1969 I was serving as a Psychological Operations (PsyOps) officer in the First Cavalry Division in Vietnam. At the time most able-bodied North Vietnamese men were in the army fighting the war in the South. China graciously sent men to fill the jobs as farmers, laborers and managers in North Vietnam.

I devised a demoralization campaign with leaflets and broad-casts asking such questions as "When you go home, who will your child call Daddy?" and "Who's been sleeping in your bed?" I considered this ingenious. Unfortunately, my boss, a Major with strong southern Christian beliefs, considered this campaign unethical. It did not get off the ground.

This experience pointed out to me the dilemma of defining ethical behavior. Certain acts are clearly unethical, but there is a very large gray area in which the ethical and the unethical are complexly defined—if at all. Cultural backgrounds, personal experiences, family morals and many other influencers define this area.

The question at hand is: How can we clearly define ethics in global sales?

The easy answer is that the company has to set the ethical standards for the salespeople. This sounds good but does not usually work. I have yet to see a mission statement that promotes unethical behavior. Companies that condone or promote what most of us would consider unethical behavior do not state that in writing. It is just a part of company culture.

The problem for the salesperson is that she is caught in the middle. The company may visibly support ethics but really wants results that require a certain amount of unethical behavior. Guess who gets fired if something goes wrong? Not the company! Their mission statement is very clear. The salesman, that dirty scoundrel, is to blame.

The problem is compounded when the company sells through distributors and a paradigm is created in which ethics can easily be delegated. The company simply maintains its strong ethical stance, but will quickly terminate a distributor who does not get sales. The company does not want to hear about unethical behavior, but the salesman has to walk a fine line between pleasing both his employer and the distributor.

An example of this is when the distributor tells the salesman that it needs an additional 5 or 10 percent "commission" or "discount" in order to get the business. The salesperson knows that this money will be used to pay a bribe, but cannot tell the company that, even though his managers know exactly what is going on. The company can then give the extra "discount" and remain ethically clean. If the situation blows up then it is the fault of the renegade salesman and the crooked distributor.

The problem for salesmen and distributors is that they have to produce results and no excuses are accepted. The problem is exacerbated when the competitor companies come from a culture in which such unethical behavior is not only condoned but perfectly acceptable and legal. Now the playing field is not level and more pressure is put on the salesman and distributor.

Some years ago I owned a company that was a distributor for a major U. S. manufacturer of compressors. We were bidding on a multi-million dollar project in a foreign country. My contact, a manager for that company, explained to me that we would have to include a 10 percent "commission" for the government oversight board in order to take part in the bid. Is this clearly unethical? That depends on whom you ask.

Our competitor, a European company had a different view of ethics at the time, a view that was supported by its country and its culture. For this company, it was perfectly legal to pay bribes (outside of Europe) and these could be deducted as a business expense. It would appear that they had the upper hand. But the plot thickened!

I asked my manager if agreeing to this "commission" would guarantee the order. The answer was that it would not. All companies had to agree to this arrangement just to be able to take part in the bid. I then asked if payment of a 15 percent commission would cement the deal and was told that the board would not accept 15 percent, only 10%. To accept 15% for the order would be unethical. Very interesting arrangement, a no-lose situation!

Another dilemma for the manufacturer and I was the veracity of what the manager was telling me. He was a very honest man, but certainly many times a distributor will use a story such as this one just to fatten its coffers, at the expense of the manufacturer. Perhaps even the company salesman is in for a cut. Unethical behavior can come at all levels.

It is fairly easy for a company that controls all levels of the sale to insure that its concept of ethical behavior is maintained. Some companies even reward ethical behavior in spite of a lost sale. A salesman has to be very wary of situations in which the company espouses ethical behavior but only rewards sales and does not want to hear excuses.

Is there a solution for the ethical salesman? The only way is to find a company that stands behind what it espouses as ethical behavior. Of course, in truth, many salesmen either have a wider view of what is ethical, or just do not care about the shackles of ethical behavior. Some of them crash and burn, but some of them are very successful. Unethical and smart is tough to compete against.

Enforcement of ethics is a top-down affair. The company that wants to be ethical has to set the rules and the culture. It has to be willing to suffer some short-term business losses in order to maintain integrity and reputation in the long term. The company that enforces its ethical standards will be rewarded for its reputation, but will always have to defend itself from the unethical competitors.

Influencers and Decision Makers in International Sales

We have all learned it in sales training. In a client company we must identify and cultivate both decision makers and influencers. Perhaps the sales trainer drew the power/influence grid. The story during the last administration was that, as President, Bill Clinton had both power and influence. Al Gore, as the elected Vice President, had authority but very little influence. But Hilary Clinton, as the First Lady, had plenty of influence, even though she was not elected and, at least officially, had no power. Unfortunately, "we the people", as is usually the case, have neither power nor influence.

Typically, the higher up the authority ladder, the greater the decision making power. Usually the influencers are "people like assistants, technicians, users and advisers," as stated by Neil Rackham in *Major Account Sales Strategy*. In the arena of global sales this division of decision makers from influencers is often turned on its head.

There is a major difference in long distance selling from the typical domestic sales relationship. In local sales often many levels in your company are involved with the selling process. Your President or Senior Manager may play golf with the top decision maker in the client company. Your technicians and service personnel may spend time after work socializing with users from client companies. Your engineers may go to the same religious services as their engineers. There may be contact with decision makers and influencers at all levels of both organizations.

In the global setting you may be the only person to have regular contact with a client company. Your senior management may stop by every few years to glad-hand, and your client's top generals may make the trip to the factory every so often. But the huge bulk of relationship maintenance falls on the broad shoulders of the global road warrior, the international sales person. You have to maintain relationships at all levels.

When I was President (believe me, that means "salesman") of a previous company my largest client for fifteen years was Paranapanema S. A. of Brazil. The President and major stockholder was Octavio Lacombe, a true Business Man of the Year in Brazil and larger-than-life person. Over the years our relationship developed from arms-length to a good friendship. In these 15 years, to the best of my recollection, he made only two decisions relative to business with my company – and these were both major purchase and tactical decisions. But while he did not generally make the decisions, he was the greatest influencer I could have.

If, however, I did not develop relationships at all levels of the company this influence would not have brought in business. I developed close relationships, and friendships with all the executives of Paranapanema. We analyzed tactics on how to best get machinery into a new mine site in the middle of the Amazon jungle and played tennis on the weekends. Of all these influencer vice presidents, only one was the direct decision-maker regarding decisions about business with my company – the General Manager of Mines. The heads of finance, construction, legal affairs, and so on were influencers on various other levels.

It is very true that the assistants, technicians, users, and advisers mentioned above were also influencers, and I had to cultivate relationships with them as well. I learned Portuguese so I could effectively interact with the engineers at the mines. I discussed parts failures with the operators of the equipment. I helped to design processing plants with the technicians. All these people were important to my business, and were strong influencers.

In the end, the real decision makers were the purchasing director and purchasing agents who made the buying decisions. But they were very strongly influenced by people in other levels of the organization who saw that I was interested in all aspects of their operation and that I took the time to learn the language and to develop personal relationships.

As you can see from this example, a global salesperson has to be a chameleon in many ways, as I suggested in an earlier chapter. I had to be able to hold my own with a charismatic leader, vice presidents, users, engineers, secretaries and so on. Neil Rachkam recognizes this later in his book when he states that "The traditional distinction between influencers and decision makers is breaking down."

In international sales it broke down millennia ago.

Vincent S. Daniels

Finding Solutions to Problems

The business buzzword nowadays seems to be "Solutions". In the business magazines, and even on television, all types of companies are offering "solutions". Some even anoint themselves as "The Solutions Company" or some similar cognomen.

Many salesmen are quick to offer pre-designed solutions to perceived problems. Most salespeople lack the skills to find out what the real problem might be, and to hold off on offering a solution until the real problem has been uncovered.

One credo to remember in order to avoid offering solutions too quickly is the one taught to psychiatrists in medical school: "The problem the patient brings you is never the real problem." The patient may have insomnia, but that is not the real problem. There is some underlying condition causing the insomnia, and it is the psychiatrist's job to assist the patient in discovering this condition.

Interpolating this to the world of sales, "the problem the client brings you is never the real problem." It is your job as a salesperson to lead the client on a mission of discovery to find the real underlying problem. Once the root of the problem is discovered a proper solution can be prescribed. If you "treat" the perceived problem you may be prescribing the wrong medicine.

So how do you go about helping the client to discover the real problem? You become an expert at questioning technique and at the art of "reversing".

Asking questions should come naturally. Salespeople have to ask questions. I discussed this earlier in the chapter, "Questions Bring More Than Answers."

Our job is to ask probing questions and to find out the real problems. Only then can we offer valid solutions.

There are basically three ways to get information: asking questions, using leading statements and reversing. Asking questions like "What kinds of problems are you having?" is a good way to start probing. But remember that the client probably does not know the real problem, so this type of questioning will only take us so far. Then we have to use leading statements like "Tell me more!" or "and…" in order to get the client to take us farther.

As salespeople, where is the "farther" we want to get to? We want to get beyond the "What is the problem?" and onward to the "Why?" Now we are getting closer to the root of the problem. Not only looking for the symptoms, but also for the reasons, the why behind the problem.

As salespeople we must also remember that clients buy based on emotion and justify the decision with facts. Searching for the "Why?" will lead us into more emotional areas than the very intellectual "What?"

These techniques of questioning are not new at all, and are not limited to sales. Every cop show on television displays interrogating techniques that follow the same pattern. If you can get behind the what, into the why, and evoke emotion, you may get valuable information, or even a confession.

I first learned these questioning techniques, including the reversing that we will look at later, when I was in "spy school" in the Army. All military intelligence personnel went through spy training at "The Bird" – Fort Holabird, Maryland. One area stressed in this school was interviewing, or interrogating techniques. Sales people can use these same techniques very effectively.

Reversing is a technique, that when mastered, will move you into the realm of "super-salesperson." You will not only be looking for the why behind the what, but exploring the impact of the problem with the client. If you can get into the area of impact, a very emotional area, you will be able to bond more strongly with your clients and greatly enhance your selling effectiveness.

There is an expression in English about "walking a mile in my shoes" in order to be able to understand my problems and what drives me. If you can walk with a client through the processes of What, Why and Impact you will begin to understand her problems. If you can understand the problems, and bring the client with you on the journey, then you will be able to offer effective solutions.

Reversing is the art of reversing someone else's question into a question of your own. In business, if someone asks you a question, there is a reason for asking it. As a salesperson the answer to the question is of little value compared to the reason the person is asking it. The reason the person asks, the "Why?" will lead to understanding the problem. You have to develop the skills to be able to follow the problem.

Remember the basic rule of reversing – no one asks you a question without a reason. If you answer the question off-hand you are missing valuable information that will help you discover the problem and make the sale. If someone asks a car salesman if this particular model comes with a standard transmission, there is a reason for the question. If the salesperson answers the question, then a rare opportunity to gather information has been passed up. The super-salesperson re-verses: "There must be a reason you are interested in a standard transmission."

Sure there is a reason, and the salesperson can only guess what it is! By reversing, you can find out. Perhaps it is to have sport car control, or for better gas mileage, or a lower sticker price, or better feel. You can only find the "Why?" behind the "What?" by reversing. When you master these techniques, you will be able to progress from the "What?" to the "Why?" to the "Impact" and on to the sale and a long-term customer—long-term because they know that you will take the time to understand the problem before you offer solutions to the symptoms!

Keeping Your Customers

Getting new customers is one crucial part of global sales. Keeping them, however, is even more important. The cost of losing a good customer is huge. It takes a psychological toll on a salesperson and a company as well as a financial toll.

Knowing that your errors led to the loss of a major account is a terrible feeling. If you have been in sales for any length of time, this has happened to you. Sometimes we blame ourselves, and sometimes we blame factors outside our control. Remember, though, that as salespeople, we always take responsibility for everything.

We need to give customers special attention in order to keep them. We all know about the many efforts we must make in order to maintain our valuable accounts. But there is one step which is often neglected, and very much feared: Bringing up problems that the customer may have with you and your company before these problems become reasons for going somewhere else.

In an earlier chapter, "Questions Bring More Than Answers," I wrote about how to find problems before you offer solutions. As salespeople our job is to find out the real problem that the client or prospect has. We then address the real problem rather than that which the customer perceives the problem to be. This is comparable to a doctor prescribing aspirin for abdominal pain without doing a thorough checkup. The pain could very well be caused by appendicitis, in which case prescribing the aspirin may be malpractice on the part of the doctor.

Unfortunately, salespeople often prescribe aspirin and fail to use good selling techniques to find out the real cause of the problem. It is the easy, unprofessional way out and is the selling equivalent of malpractice. But the salesperson should not stop at just finding the cause of the problem. The next step, and the harder one, is to discover the effect that this problem is having on the company and the person involved. This takes good selling skills.

Business decisions are generally made on the basis of avoiding the pain associated with an existing or potential problem. Only by knowing the effects of the problems, and the pain these can cause, can we truly effective at sales. In other words, we salespeople have to make the effort to truly know our customers—even better than they know themselves.

Now let's return to the topic of how to keep clients. To do this, we have to take the selling technique of finding the problem and its effects and use it on ourselves and our own company. To reprise the medical metaphor, this is the equivalent of going to the doctor for an annual checkup. We hope he will find nothing, but we want to know early if there is a potential problem.

On a regular basis we need to find out from our clients what problems related to our business relationship with them might be on the horizon. We usually have no idea what this problem may be, or even if there is one.

However, sometimes a problem comes up and we have to go into emergency mode to find out what can be done to fix the problem and keep an upset or irate customer happy. Here is a technique you may want to use on a regular, annual checkup type basis. It can also be used in those emergency situations.

I compare finding a problem and its effects, and perhaps the pains that these effects are causing to a volcano. If we see a volcanic island we can identify it by several indicators. Perhaps we see smoke or a red glow at the top. Maybe there is lava pouring down the side and into the ocean. At least we see the conical shape of the volcano. These are all indicators of a volcano.

Customers' problems usually also have indicators. It may be reduced orders, or allowing a new supplier to bid, or a complaint about service. Remember that, as salespeople, we always take responsibility for any problem the customer may have with our company.

Just like the volcano indicators, the sales indicators are often very clear, but they do not point to the source of the problem. In the case of the volcano the source is a crack in the earth's crust many miles below the surface of the ocean. The real problem of the customer is only indicated by the obvious signs. We have to dig deep to find the real problems and their effects on the customer's business.

Once or twice a year we should run a preventive maintenance checkup with our clients. We have to ask the question to our customers, often asked by former Mayor Koch in New York – "How are we doing?" But we can't stop there. The client will often say that we are doing just great, but that may not be entirely true. Or she may not be thinking of the problems at that moment. We have to take it a step further.

A good way to approach this is to ask a question like, "I appreciate your confidence in us, and am glad that everything is okay, but there is always room for improvement. If there were one area that we could improve, what would that be?" Or if we are aware of a potential problem, we can bring it up. "Some other clients have told me that shipments sometimes arrive broken. I don't suppose that you have encountered this problem".

Search hard for actual or potential problems. Have them talk about it. Look for the effects that the problem has or may have on their business. After you have gone through a full discovery process you can begin to search for a good solution, and perhaps help to mitigate the effects of the problem. Find potential problems yourself or, I guarantee, your competitors will find them. If they have good sales skills, they will steal your clients.

It is much more expensive to find a new client than to keep an existing one. Do your preventive maintenance (your annual checkup) and you will keep clients happier and keep them for longer.

The Trade Show

Cultural and Security Considerations

One of the most time- and resource-consuming sales events for a company is the trade show. In global sales, this time and resource consumption is compounded by distance, shipping, customs, and a host of other variables.

Trade shows present a unique opportunity in which you and your management team can meet with customers, suppliers and competitors in a very intense format. Some industries have only one major show a year, while some become a traveling circus with shows nearly every week. Their success depends on careful planning, effective attendance, and an organized follow-up. In this article, I will cover important considerations in planning for the show. Later on in this article, I cover preparation, what to do at the show and how to follow up effectively—that is, sales both during and after the trade show (not logistics).

International trade shows are particularly challenging not only because of distance and logistics, but also because they occur in different cultures. Each region and country has differing trade show customs; industries also have different cultures. Sometimes you can play these cultural differences to your advantage.

Most of my experience has been in the Americas and Europe, particularly Germany, and comes from the equipment industry, although I also have taken part in high-tech and apparel shows.

If it's your first time attending a particular show, be sure to talk with people who already have had experience. You will need to know how to fit into that particular culture so that you don't stick out like a sore thumb. In Germany, for example, you had best have a "gasthaus" attached to your booth. This is a place that will serve beer and schnapps, and some food to go with it, such as wurst and potato salad. If you do not include these amenities in your display area, you will not get very many visitors. This spot usually takes the place of a "hospitality room" prevalent at many U. S. shows.

I attended a show in Argentina that included a few German companies. They brought their Warsteiner and Weisswurst with them, but quickly realized that this was not a part of the show culture in Buenos Aires. In this case the German culture prevailed, and, although they kept the goodies in a back room, they had more visitors than anyone else.

Learning about the culture is a part of the overall planning process.

When I was in military intelligence a long time ago, we could put a transmitter into a martini olive. I have no idea what may be available today. We had a training program called DASE – Defense Against Surveillance Equipment. Of course, the best defense is a good offense, so the course taught agents how to prepare and use this equipment. (The name also helped in keeping congressmen quiet.) I suggest that your company have someone in-house or an outside consultant to help you to make sure that your trade show safe-rooms are truly safe. And, make sure to not use the same consultant your competitors are using.

Ensuring security and confidentiality regarding your business deals while at the trade show is another part of the overall planning process. In addition, most exhibitors and customers will show up with a host of senior people and decision makers. This fact presents an excellent opportunity for top executives to get together, to bond, and to make deals. The problem is that these shows are very public. Everyone knows who is visiting whom and what deals are in the works: Industrial espionage made easy!

In an exhibition hall there usually is no security for your booth. Anyone can go in after-hours and steal brochures and products, go through trash cans, and plant bugs. Companies hire outside security firms or do it themselves.

I have seen many companies with meeting rooms in their booths, where important meetings with clients and suppliers are held. This is insanity! These rooms are far too public and accessible. They are also much too easy to bug with eavesdropping devices.

In many U. S. shows, exhibitors (and sometimes users) reserve hospitality rooms in nearby hotels to entertain prospects and customers. While they offer a greater degree of confidentiality, as they are typically "by invitation only," these rooms are still very open and public places. The best bet is to reserve another room for private meetings. This room could be in the same hotel but on a different floor than where the trade show is located. This room should be scheduled well in advance for meetings specifically designed to close deals. It's where you will come after the golf game.

Many companies are too small to afford hospitality rooms or private meeting rooms, or are new to market and do not have high-level meetings to set up. In those cases, you will have to meet in your booth or in one of the meeting areas provided by the administrators of the show. Here are some security precautions that you can take: Always remember that you are in public view. When you identify good prospects, try to set up a meeting away from the show—perhaps a meal or a visit to their offices would be possible.

The next section will discuss how to plan organizationally for the show, including how to use incentives such as prize drawings to your best advantage. I will then cover follow up and other loose ends.

The Trade Show: Preparation

First, you must have a "people" plan. You will spend a lot of money and other resources in attending a trade show, especially if it is a major industry event in another country. A major show is like a positive alignment of the stars. You will have your senior management in attendance. Clients will bring in their senior management to visit with suppliers and see the most current developments in their industry. You cannot let this singular opportunity go to waste.

If you have important deals in the works, or you have key clients to develop, the trade show is the perfect venue to jump forward in leaps and bounds. Develop a schedule for your key people. Of course, they will need time to see the show and to meet with people on the floor, but their most valuable time, from your viewpoint as the salesman, will be in small group meetings with the key managers of client companies.

These meetings should take place away from the display booth. You can use the separate meeting room that you reserved ahead of time, go to a breakfast, lunch or dinner, or visit the golf course. Try to prearrange as many meals as possible between your key people and the clients. Work your bosses to the bone. A trade show is not a place for fun and games and wasted time. Use every opportunity that you can.

Next, you have to have a booth-manning plan. Someone must always be there. How many people will have to be there at any time will depend on the size of your company and the number of product lines you have. You should always have people available who can give basic information on any of your products. If you qualify a visitor as a potential client who needs more detailed information, you should set up a meeting with a specialist. You should have a manning roster available so that a meeting can easily be set up when the specialist will be in the booth.

Next is a personnel plan for readiness and strategy. It is amazing how much time and money companies spend in planning and designing a display for a trade show. Then there are the additional costs in time and money in shipping, setting up, and breaking down the booth. It is equally amazing to me how little time is typically spent in preparing the personnel to take part in the show. There is usually little common strategy, and woefully few established objectives.

Set up a series of meetings well before the show to establish overall objectives, as well as objectives for each participant. On a person-by-person and department-by-department basis these objectives may be related to meeting customers, closing deals, getting leads, or unveiling new products or services. You may be interested in exposing your company to a new market, or to finding new suppliers, or to negotiating better terms with existing suppliers. Whatever they may be, they have to be discussed and understood by all.

These objectives should not be only conceptual. Once the various objectives have been ascertained, goals should be set.

Only if goals are set will concrete results be achieved. If one goal is for the CEO to meet with major clients, a goal should be set as to how many clients will be met, and what the outcome of the meetings should be. If your goal is to qualify/disqualify 50 prospects, then you have to take steps to insure that at least 50 prospects will visit your display, and that you will have sufficient personnel on hand to go through the process.

The objectives and goals should be discussed and agreed to by all parties concerned in advance. The final step in preparing for the show is marketing. Then the pre-show meetings and marketing should be designed to guarantee that these goals can be met.

Now that the objectives and goals have been set you have to attract the right people to your booth. Target your invitations and your advertising. Make calls and send emails to all the right people. Your very important individual meetings may be established in advance, if this was one objective. But you probably need new prospects if the show is to be a success. You may also want to invite smaller customers that do not warrant a private meeting. Whatever you do, market to the objectives and goals you have set.

All types of gimmicks are used to draw prospects into the tent. Depending on the culture of the show it could be beautiful women, celebrities, giveaways, food and drinks or business card drop-in raffles. This is not even the beginning of an all-inclusive list. The list could go on as far as the imagination can take it. Just remember that the gimmick you use should work towards the objectives and goals you have set.

The business card raffle is often used, and can be a very effective marketing tool. Whatever lure you use, you must have your salespeople trained in how to quickly qualify or disqualify walk-ins. The pace of selling at a show is much faster than that of a typical sales call. You have to qualify quickly and get pertinent information so you can have an effective follow-up.

At times you will be inundated with walk-ins. You cannot spend too much time with any one, and you must disqualify the tourists quickly, no matter how beautiful or handsome they may be. Set up dry runs before the show to practice your questioning techniques to insure good qualifying practices. Practice writing notes on the backs of the business cards or elsewhere so you will remember the pertinent details about qualified visitors. Set up future meetings as possible. Make the most of the limited time you will have available for each person. The show will be over before you know it.

The Importance of Follow-up After a Trade Show

In the last two sections we went through the preparation and execution of a major international trade show. We now come to the most crucial part, the follow-up. Too many companies spend time and money on having a successful trade show and then drop the ball on the follow-up.

At the end of the trade show, if it was worked properly, everyone involved is experiencing a mix of feelings – exhaustion, exhilaration, satisfaction, and/or frustration. The last thing we want to do is get back to the routine. But the routine is calling. You have been out of the office for a week or so. What has happened? The work you are normally there to do has been piling up. There are emergencies to take care of. Personal obligations are also demanding attention. You are inundated with work.

So what happens to the follow-up of the trade show? It is put off until you have a chance to catch up. And after two or three weeks of catching up, the memories have faded and the time-liness of a contact has passed. You have wasted much of the trade show effort.

As a salesperson or sales manager you have to have a plan **before** the trade show begins on how you will execute the follow up. You must allocate time immediately after the trade show to follow-up with the contacts you made. Hopefully, you have categorized them into priorities so you can take care of the hottest and best leads first.

If need be, get some help. There are probably chores such as database entry and mailings that can be done by someone else. You may have to hire a temp, or bring in a student intern to help with the follow-up chores. Build these extras into the cost of the trade show.

After the trade show you should make contact with the best leads right away. Continue interviewing and qualifying them in a more detailed way than you could during the hustle and bustle of the trade show floor. Get quotations out if they were requested. Set up meetings if this is practical, or involve your local agent or distributor in the process. The door is open now for developing a business relationship, but it closes more each day that the contact is put off.

For the leads that were qualified at the trade show, but which do not warrant a call or visit right away, get something in the mail or by email to them right away. Move while the memory is still fresh. If you have local agents or distributors, alert them to these leads.

The trade show tourists that you disqualified can now be discarded. You do not have time for these. Spend your time on real-live prospects.

If you had a gimmick like a business card raffle, now is the time to make use of it. This method is one of the most used and most effective methods of gleaning new prospects at a trade show. Basically, you draw people into the booth by offering a prize for a business card that will be drawn at random from a receptacle used to collect the cards. The best is some sort of a fish bowl that allows the cards to be seen.

Once again, the people manning the booth have to be trained in how to use this gimmick to the best advantage. The time when the prospect comes into the booth to deposit the card into the fish bowl is the only chance you may have to qualify or disqualify. The booth personnel must be trained and should attempt to qualify every card that is deposited. The best method to do this is to make some notes on the back of the card before it is thrown in. Another method is to request a second card and to put notes on it.

The prize should be something desirable, but not too expensive. It should be something that can be delivered by hand. If possible, it should be a product you produce or distribute, or something pertinent to your business. I worked with a computer manufacturer once in preparing for a trade show and we settled on a good quality video board. This fit all of the above prerequisites. In the global marketplace we also have to think about shipping costs, importation problems, and such that could restrict our ability to deliver the prize. Perhaps the prize would have to be delivered by a distributor or agent or on your next trip.

Now comes the question of who gets the prize. Unfortunately, a random drawing is, by definition, random. I have known some companies who pick a well-qualified prospect to win the prize. You have to have a very low ethics threshold in your company if you resort to this, but many companies are not concerned with ethical issues. I find this to be unfortunate. A lack of ethics will usually come back to haunt you.

If you followed the guidelines of the perfect prize – good quality, desirable, not too expensive, pertinent and portable – then you have a good alternative. Build your budget for more than one prize. You can then draw a winner randomly, fulfilling your ethical obligation, and then select other "winners" to receive the prize, also. Some of you may find this also to be unethical. If so, do not use this tactic. Everyone's ethical threshold is different.

Now, with prizes in hand, you have a good reason for getting a face-to-face meeting with the prospect – to deliver his prize. If his or her gatekeeper tries to block you, you have a good retort. The winner has to receive and sign for the prize personally. The winner has to sign a receipt stating that the gift is a prize from a raffle and in no way incurs any obligation for future business. Explain that this is an ethics requirement of your company. (Are we close to anyone's threshold here?)

To sum it up, there are three post-trade show imperatives:

1. The follow-up to the trade show must be pre-planned and budgeted.

2. Do not get sidetracked by the work that has built up in your absence; have a plan in place on how to take care of this.

3. Do not waste the time and money spent on the trade show by not having a good follow-up plan.

Team Selling

Often the sales call in a global setting is done by a team of people. The team may consist of the salesperson in charge of the account, a technical person, a finance person, and a sales manager. It may be a salesman, a distributor salesperson or agent and a manager from home office, or any other combination. It is very possible that the team meets formally for only a brief period immediately before the sales call. Perhaps the team members are from totally different areas geographically. With all of these factors in play, how can you maintain control of the meeting and insure that it progresses to the desired outcome?

First, let's start with why it is important for you to control the meeting. It is very easy for the client or prospect to take control of the meeting and use it to his own advantage. As salespeople we want to maintain control and not give away too much free consulting. We want to make a sale, not give the client more ammunition to be able to shop around with a greater level of knowledge than he had before we arrived.

There are some steps to take and to enforce in order to insure a successful outcome to a team sales call.

As with any other sales call, the first step is to plan in advance. Decide what you want to accomplish and what strategy you will use to guide you. You also have to inform your client, as well as your team, what the objectives are. Very briefly, you have to enter into an agreement with your client. In the case of a team call you also have to have agreement among the team members. The basis agreement with the client and with the team includes:

- Set an agenda for the meeting. What do you plan to cover?
- What will you and your team members need to do? Obviously, you will need to ask questions, but it is best to advise what types of questions you plan to ask (budget, decision process, problems, etc.). Ask permission in advance to ask the required questions. You may also need a room to work in, or access to data or decision makers. Stipulate what the role of you and your team will be.
- What does your client have to do to prepare for the meeting, and what is their role during the meeting? Perhaps they have to set up site visits and arrange for transportation, or have certain materials ready for testing or inspection. Of course, give them permission to ask questions. Every question they may ask is an indicator to a possible problem they have.
- Set the desired outcome of the meeting.
- Put objections that you foresee on the table early so they can be overcome (or not overcome) before you get too far into the sales process.
- Verbalize any fears you may have. Do not give the client an opportunity to play games with you.

Include your team members in developing this pre-meeting agreement. Make sure that you establish yourself as team leader, or make certain that the team leader knows what is involved in that role. He may not have read this article.

A major problem with team selling is that the client can get the team members to play against one another to seek an advantage. With or without the client's prodding, one team member may say something that is detrimental to the overall strategy of the team leader. It is the Caesarean concept of "divide and conquer".

There are a number of important steps that can be taken to minimize these negative possibilities.

First, have a physical meeting of all the team members prior to the sales call. If an outside member, such as a distributor salesperson or agent, will take part in the meeting, have an insider meeting first. You may need to have a strategy session during the meeting to decide how to deal with the outside member. Only after the strategy is developed, include the outside member. This may turn out to be a sales negotiation before the real negotiation begins with the end-user.

Next, assign the roles of the team members. One member should be the team leader and should be responsible for following the sales strategy. If possible, appoint one person to be the silent member. This member can keep notes and remain non-emotional in the sales process. He can be the referee in case other team members go off course in the heat of the negotiation.

Stress that no one should answer questions without the permission of the team leader. The team leader must be well-schooled in questioning techniques, especially reversing.

The team leader should take over early in the process. At the beginning of the meeting, after the customary niceties, the team leader should review the agenda, roles and desired outcome of the meeting. This establishes the team leader as spokesman for the group at the very start of the meeting.

All eyes should be on him . This is an excellent use of non-verbal communication. If all team members' eyes and attention are on the leader, the proper message is sent. Also, it is much more difficult for the clients to address other members of the team when the only eye contact is with the team leader. Eye contact opens the door for direct questions; so let only the team leader maintain eye contact with the clients.

The team leader can then direct certain questions to other team members as required. "Also, Frank has some specific questions relative to operating efficiency. Would it be okay if he asks them now?" The baton has been passed. Now all team members' eyes and attention transfer to Frank. He had better have some well-rehearsed questions to pose, with no surprises to other team members.

When Frank is finished he passes the baton back to the team leader. "Thanks for the information. Now I think that Joan has some additional items to cover." The baton is passed back to the team leader.

Should the client direct a question directly to the silent member, or a member other than the team leader there are several options to maintain control. Either the team leader can jump in and reverse the question, or the other member can begin to field the question and then, in mid answer, send it back to the team leader. He can also look for a non-verbal cue from the team leader that it is okay, or not okay, to go ahead with an answer. Team members should only issue answers that have been prepared ahead of time. Otherwise, the team leader should reverse the question in order to probe for potential problems the client may have. Remember, every time a client or prospect asks a question he has a very good reason for asking it. It is the salesperson's duty to find out what the reason is. It is also the salesperson's right to ask a reversing question any time an answer is given to a client. Always find out the reason the question was asked. The team leader should be a master of questioning technique.

At the end of the team sales call the leader should review any actions that need to be taken by team members. This is to insure that each team member has taken ownership of her responsibilities as a follow up to the meeting. After the meeting an action plan can be drawn up and discussed to insure understanding and compliance by all team members. If decisions have been made during the sales visit, these should also be reviewed. It is very easy for team members to forget decisions that have been made during a meeting. Also, these should be reviewed with the client to reinforce decisions that he has made or agreed to. This step will help to avoid misinterpretations after the meeting.

Follow up on the meeting with a letter or email from the team leader. This letter should thank the client for inviting the team in, and should summarize the actions that need to be taken by both parties and the decisions that were made during the meeting.

Vincent S. Daniels

The Ultimate Global Road Warrior

When a salesperson is on the road, it is interesting to observer our colleagues. I also call this gathering intelligence. One of the most interesting places to see how different competitors and cultures prepare for an important sales call is in the breakfast room of a hotel. Many international salesmen have told me about certain behaviors that now seem to me to be a pattern.

The final planning for the big customer visit is done over breakfast. The restaurant is the final staging ground. The players meet to finalize objectives and roles and to polish their presentation.

Typically, the Japanese sales team needs a large table. There may be as many as five or six team members. There may be a high-ranking technician, a service support manager, a financial wiz, a parts guru, a regional salesman, and high-ranking decision maker to pull it all together. They all have important roles to play in this compartmentalized team, although the key importance of some of these roles may only be their presence.

The Europeans may need only a table for four. The team may consist of two to four people, usually a technical person, the responsible salesman, a service support guy and a senior manager. (The designated genders are also typical.)

Over in his corner, ("her corner" is becoming more and more prevalent,) reading the regional international edition of the Herald Tribune is the American salesperson, the ultimate global road warrior.

Why are there such different approaches to international sales? I do not claim to have the answer for all the examples. For the American salesperson, however, I do have a theory.

At the turn of the last century, in 1900, financier Edward Tuck made a generous contribution to Dartmouth College to start a five-year academic program for the study of business. Today, this is the renowned Tuck School of Business. In the first three years, students worked toward acquiring a bachelor's degree; in the next two years, they progressed toward a master's degree. In 1902, seven young men earned the Master of Commercial Science diploma, the predecessor to the Master of Business Administration, from the Tuck School.

Some years later, the United States entered into the First World War in Europe. This experience opened the eyes of future American businessmen and educators to the world market. Many graduate programs of business began adding international and import/export courses. International business education began to develop.

Slowly, the programs gathered around the MBA name. But within this name were many flavors of an MBA. Some were generalist in nature, churning out our business managers, while others became specialized; for example, a financial MBA program to supply Wall Street with analysts.

In the 1940s, the United States was engaged in the Second World War, which introduced future businessmen to the Pacific and Atlantic cultures. The U.S. also became the dominant world industrial power largely as a result of the industrial buildup for the war, and the fact that our industrial infrastructure was not destroyed as a result of the war. More internationally-oriented businessmen were urgently needed.

In the mid 1940s, several colonels who were retiring after the war convinced General Barton Kyle Yount, Commanding General, Army Air Forces Training Command, that Americans needed to be educated in international business. He acquired an Army Air Corps training base (Thunderbird Field) in the Arizona desert and founded Thunderbird, then called the American Institute of Foreign Trade. This was the first school dedicated to the teaching of international business.

In the early 1970s, Thunderbird transformed itself into a graduate school offering the Master of International Management (now the MBA in International Management) diploma. Hence, the Global Road Warriors concept began. (This was a free advertising plug for my Alma Mater.)

The purpose of these internationally oriented MBA programs is to turn our globally savvy managers. In addition, many times the route to senior management leads through the sales channel. Therefore, those of you currently in sales with aspirations for senior management should heed this advice.

American MBA programs are typically general in scope, providing learning in marketing, finance, management, organizational design, information technology and systems, and international business environment. This list is not all-inclusive, as now many schools offer varying international MBA degrees.

Also, the MBA is not just for business undergraduates. Many MBA candidates have technical or engineering degrees, but any undergraduate degree can lead to an international MBA. For example, an International MBA student who has a classical music undergraduate may have a future as president of a musical instrument manufacturer, or director of a major orchestra that plays all over the world. This exemplifies how a technical background is actually a strong asset for the global businessperson.

Remember the Japanese team from the beginning of this article? Now look at the preceding paragraph. The MBA program, with origins and concept in the United States has been able to reproduce the team in one individual. This person can discuss finance, supply chain management, and IT, and is probably empowered with the authority to make changes and take decisions. That is the power of the MBA-educated salesperson.

The salesperson with an International MBA is also culturally adept. He probably speaks several languages and can operate with minimum support anywhere in the world! In short, he is a power to be reckoned with: A Global Road Warrior!

Of course, success leads to imitation. Business people from every country in the world have come to the U.S. for an MBA degree. Now MBA education is proliferating throughout Europe and the rest of the world. Perhaps we are seeing smaller teams at the breakfast table, especially with the high cost of international travel.

As corporations become more global in their scope and management mix there is much more need for internationally oriented talent. The International MBA will continue to grow throughout the world because the need is there.

Printed in the United States
33990LVS00006B/16-42